Deer in the New Forest

JOHN JACKSON

MOONRAKER PRESS

Key to Map

1 HALE PURLIEU
2 CASTLE HILL AND GODSHILL IS.
3 MILLERSFORD PLANTATION AND TURF HILL
4 ASHLEY WALK
5 FRANCHISES WOOD
6 BRAMSHAW I. AND WOOD
7 RAVENS NEST I. AND BROOM HILL
8 COPPICE OF LINWOOD AND SALISBURY TRENCH IS.
9 ISLAND THORN I. AND EYEWORTH
10 PITTS WOOD I.
11 HAMPTON RIDGE AND LATCHMOOR BOTTOM
12 AMBERWOOD AND ALDERHILL IS.
13 SLODEN I.
14 HASLEY I.
15 IBSLEY COMMON
16 BROOMY AND HOLLY HATCH IS.
17 NORTH AND SOUTH BENTLEY IS.
18 KINGS GARN GUTTER AND LONG BEECH IS.
19 BIGNELL WOOD
20 OCKNELL I.
21 SLUFTER I.
22 MILKHAM AND ROE IS.
23 APPLESLADE I.
24 ROCKFORD COMMON
25 GREAT LINFORD I.
26 PINNICK WOOD
27 BISTERNE COMMON
28 DUR HILL DOWN I.
29 CRANES MOOR
30 RIDLEY WOOD
31 SOUTH OAKLEY I. AND BERRY WOOD
32 BURLEY OUTER RAILS I.
33 BACKLEY
34 BRATLEY WOOD AND I.
35 BOLDERWOOD HOLLIES
36 BOLDERWOOD SANCTUARY
37 BOLDERWOOD I.
38 NORTH OAKLEY I.
39 MARK ASH WOOD
40 ANDERWOOD I.
41 KNIGHTWOOD I.
42 HOLIDAY HILL I.
43 HOLMHILL I.
44 WOODCRATES
45 ACRES DOWN
46 HIGHLAND WATER I.
47 WITHYBEDS
48 THE GROVE
49 MANOR WOOD
50 SHAVE GREEN I. AND SHAVE WOOD
51 BROCKISHILL AND FURZEY LAWN IS.
52 RUSHPOLE WOOD
53 BUSKETTS LAWN, BUSKETTS, COSTICLES, LODGEHILL AND IRONSHILL IS.
54 CHURCHPLACE AND DEERLEAP IS.
55 LONGDOWN I.
56 IPLEY I.
57 IPLEY MANOR
58 MALLARD WOOD
59 PONDHEAD I.
60 DENNY NEW AND MATLEY IS.
61 DENNY WOOD
62 BISHOP OF WINCHESTERS PURLIEU
63 DENNY LODGE AND WOODFIDLEY IS.
64 STUBBY COPSE I.
65 PERRYWOOD HASELEY I.
66 PIGNAL I.
67 RAMNOR I.
68 PARKHILL I.
69 PARKGROUNDS I.
70 BALMER LAWN AND HOLLANDS WOOD
71 NEW PARK FARM
72 WHITLEY WOOD
73 HURSTHILL I.
74 BRICK KILN I.
75 GRITNAM WOOD
76 BRINKERN WOOD
77 VINNEY RIDGE I.
78 POUNDHILL I.
79 OBER HEATH
80 ALDRIDGEHILL I.
81 RHINEFIELD-SANDYS I.
82 DAMES SLOUGH I.
83 BURLEY LODGE
84 BURLEY NEW I.
85 BURLEY OLD I.
86 STAG BREAK AND MILLAWN
87 MARKWAY I.
88 GOATSPEN PLAIN
89 SHIRLEY COMMON
90 HOLMSLEY I.
91 WOOTTON COPPICE AND BROWNHILL IS.
92 WILVERLEY I.
93 SET THORNS I.
94 HINCHELSEA
95 RHINEFIELD
96 NEW COPSE I.
97 PERRYWOOD IRONSHILL I.
98 NORLEY I.
99 BEAULIEU HEATH
100 FRAME I.
101 STOCKLEY AND HAWKHILL IS.
102 STUBBS AND TANTANY WOODS
103 KINGS HAT, CRABHAT AND FOXHUNTING IS.
104 MARCHWOOD I.
105 DIBDEN I.
106 FAWLEY I.
107 HOLBURY PURLIEU
108 KINGS COPSE I.

I = Inclosure(s)

A ASHURST
B BURLEY
BL BLACKFIELD
BR BROCKENHURST
D DIBDEN
EB EAST BOLDRE
F FRITHAM
L LYNDHURST
M MINSTEAD
S SWAY

First published in 1977 by Moonraker Press
26 St Margarets Street, Bradford-on-Avon, Wiltshire
SBN 239 00170 2
Text set in 10/11 pt 'Monotype' Times New Roman and printed letterpress at The Pitman Press, Bath. Bound in England at The Pitman Press.

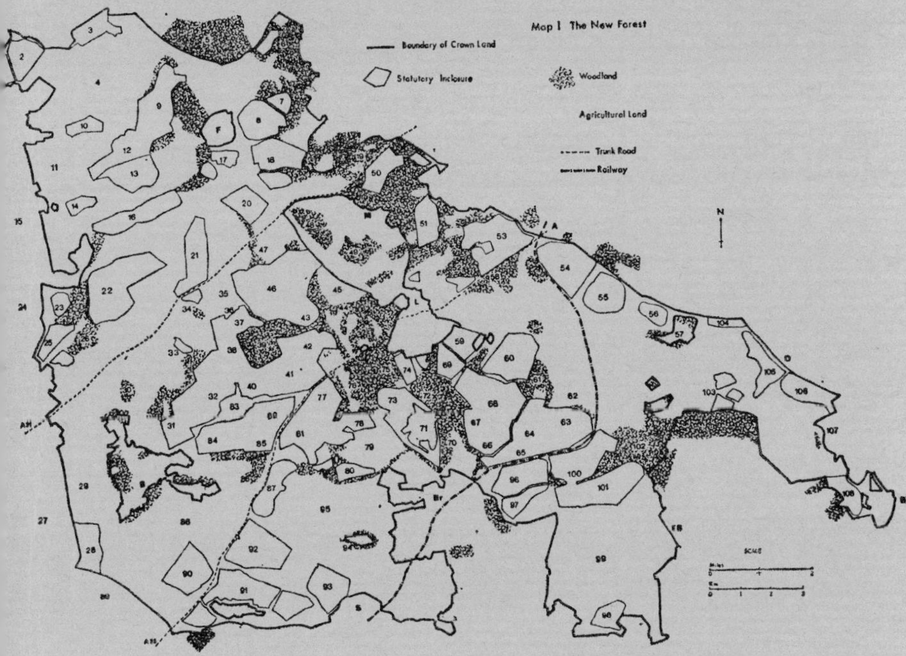

Acknowledgements

It is a pleasure to thank publicly the following who, in one way or another, helped to produce this work: Roy Worsfold who took all the photographs except no. 4; Dr D. Chapman, Norma Chapman and Fred Courtier who assisted in the preparation of the text; and the numerous local people and Forestry Commission employees—especially the entire Wildlife staff—whose understanding, guidance and friendship made my studies on the deer of the New Forest feasible.

JOHN JACKSON

The New Forest

The New Forest, which covers over 100 square miles, forms the greater part of the south-western portion of the county of Hampshire in central-southern England. To-day, five species of deer inhabit the New Forest: fallow (*Dama dama*), sika (*Cervus nippon*), roe (*Capreolus capreolus*), muntjac (*Muntiacus reevesi*) and red deer (*Cervus elaphus*).

Historians generally agree that William the Conqueror declared the New Forest a royal hunting reserve some time between 1066 and 1086. Before his death in 1087 he framed the Forest Laws which were designed to protect the game and which carried harsh penalties for poaching. In common with other royal forests in England, the New Forest was subjected to these laws for several centuries. During this period, many noblemen hunted game in the Forest and some lost their lives there. The most famous of these was the Conqueror's own son, William Rufus, who was shot through the heart by the French knight, Sir Walter Tyrrell, while pursuing deer.

Gradually through the centuries timber rather than game became of increasing importance and extensive areas were enclosed for forestry purposes. Hunting by noblemen declined and in 1851, under the New Forest Deer Removal Act, the Crown finally surrendered its right to keep deer there. This Act also provided for the total extermination of all deer in the region within two years. Fortunately this objective was never completely achieved although the herds were undoubtedly decimated. In 1923, management of the New Forest was transferred to the Forestry Commission and it became a State Forest.

Geologically, the New Forest consists of a series of plateaux, which in the north have been eroded into a system of wide valleys separated by ridges, while in the south they form expansive undulating plains which slope gently towards the sea. The highest point, 127 metres (418 ft) above sea-level, is in the extreme north of the Forest at Bramshaw Telegraph; the lowest, below 60 metres (200 ft), is on the southern border near Beaulieu. The climate of the region is mild compared with most places in Britain, especially during the winter. Average rainfall is 840 mm (33 in.) a year, of which two-thirds falls between October and March. From April through to September evaporation tends to exceed precipitation and by late summer the Forest is often tinder-dry.

The New Forest is the largest area of semi-natural vegetation remaining in lowland Britain. Largely as a result of being subjected to various management-practices extending over many centuries, the area has become a complex mosaic of semi-natural vegetation, forestry plantations and agricultural land. The Crown Land, administered by the Forestry Commission, covers about 27,000 hectares (67,000 acres), or just over 100 square miles. Two-thirds of this is unenclosed or Open Forest, composed of extensive tracts of deciduous woodland, heather moor, wet heath, bog, bracken and gorse-brakes with smaller areas of natural and re-seeded grasslands, Scots pine, holly stands and alder carrs. Fenced plantations, the Inclosures, cover the remaining third of the Forest; within them a mixture of both hard- and soft-woods of various ages are found creating an attractive, varied patchwork. Rich pastureland is scattered in pockets throughout the New Forest and adjoins much of its borders (*see* map).

The resident human population is sparse compared with much of the country, being concentrated in the villages of Burley, Fritham, Lyndhurst and Minstead within the Forest and those adjacent to the boundary or perambulation such as Ashurst, Blackfield, Brockenhurst, Dibden, East Boldre and Sway. However, vast numbers of campers and visitors are attracted to the Forest, especially during the main holiday period. Each year now some 750,000 camper-nights (one person camping for one night) are recorded and upwards of four million day-visitors use the New Forest for a variety of recreational purposes. Although walkers are allowed to go anywhere in the Forest, both on the Open Forest and in Inclosures, vehicular access is strictly limited. The public may not take vehicles into car-free zones or plantations. By-laws are displayed at various places throughout the Forest requesting people to close gates, avoid dropping litter, starting fires or feeding animals and damaging the delicate fabric of the Forest. All dogs must be kept under close control. Camping and caravanning on Crown Land is allowed only on designated camp sites; permits must be obtained from the Forestry Commission permit-offices.

Common rights are attached to many of the properties in and adjoining the New Forest. Among these ancient privileges is the right to graze commonable animals, i.e. ponies, cattle and donkeys, on the Open Forest throughout the year. Commoners may also turn out pigs during autumn and early winter to feed on the fallen acorns and beech-mast, a practice known as pannage. The hardy New Forest pony is one of the nine wild native breeds in Britain. Their origin is unknown but they are certainly of very ancient stock and were present in pre-Norman times, being mentioned in the early code 'Constitutiones de Foresta'. During the summer the combined number of ponies and cattle roaming free in the Forest approaches 5,000. Responsibility for the welfare of the commonable animals rests with the Verderers and their servants, the Agisters.

Among the many and varied responsibilities of the Forestry Commission is that of managing the wildlife. This is carried out by 13 Keepers and Rangers, and two Head Keepers under a Head Forester. At present, the Forest is divided into 12 beats, each one controlled by a keeper.

The Deer

The deer in the Forest are wild animals and in most places are free to move in and out of the area, as there is no restricting boundary fence; passage of animals to and from other wild herds in neighbouring parts of Hampshire and Wiltshire undoubtedly occurs.

Of the five species, the *Fallow deer* is the commonest. These animals are not native to the British Isles, probably being indigenous to Asia Minor. Fallow have been widely introduced by man into many parts of the world and are now found in all continents except Antarctica. This species is widely distributed in Britain nowadays, having been reported from nearly all of the English, several Scottish and most of the Welsh and Irish counties. The majority of present herds are descended from park animals which have escaped and turned feral. Those in the New Forest however are of ancient stock; their original introduction is variously attributed to the Romans, Phoenicians and Gauls but they were probably released by the Normans; fallow have lived there continuously ever since.

Some interesting information has been published on the size of the population of New Forest fallow in the past. Early censuses before 1800, when deer were still preserved, indicated that the number of fallow fluctuated between four and eight thousand but heavy winter mortality occurred in certain years. By 1850, the number of fallow had been reduced to 3,500. In 1851, the notorious New Forest Deer Removal Act was passed; the deer were decimated but were never completely exterminated. Numbers began to increase slowly again and there were estimated to be between 200 and 250 in 1892. After the Second World War the fallow population was believed to be about 450 animals. Nowadays the number of fallow has increased still further and is about 800 to 900. Fallow deer can be found over most of the New Forest although few live in the extreme south or south-east.

During the Middle Ages, *Roe deer* probably became extinct in England with the exception of the Border Counties. The roe deer in southern England today have resulted from the successful reintroduction of animals into several localities during the nineteenth and twentieth centuries, whose descendants have radiated outwards to occupy new territories. This species has undergone a tremendous population explosion this century; their numbers have increased greatly and still they are expanding their range. In the New Forest, roe re-colonised the area from 1890 onwards, spreading across from Dorset where some had been released at Milton Abbas in 1800. Roe may now be found over the whole Forest though they are scarce in certain places. Census-returns in the past ten years indicate that the roe population fluctuates considerably but averages 400–500 head. Small woodland deer, such as the roe, are notoriously difficult to count accurately however and these figures are probably an underestimate of the true numbers.

The *Sika deer* is an alien to Great Britain, its original home being eastern Asia. The sika in the New Forest, which are of the Japanese race, are descendants of four animals liberated on the Beaulieu Manor Estate to the south of the Forest in 1904 and 1905. These deer established themselves very successfully and their progeny quickly spread northwards to colonise the southern extremity of the Forest. The present herds within the Forest contain about 80 deer and are found to the south of the main Southampton-to-Bournemouth railway-line in the vicinity of New Copse, Hawkhill and Stockley Inclosures.

Red deer, which in the distant past were probably the original native deer in the Forest, never seem to have flourished to the same extent that the fallow have done. During the past 200 years their numbers do not ever appear to have exceeded 80 animals. The present number is believed to be under 40 animals, scattered in several widely distributed haunts.

Muntjac are indigenous to south-eastern Asia and were originally liberated in Britain at Woburn Park about 1900. With the help of further escapes from private collections, this species spread to colonise and become established in many suitable rural and suburban habitats in the central block of England; their range is still expanding. During the past decade, a handful of reliable observers have reported occasional sightings of the small, secretive muntjac in the New Forest. Confirmed records now exist for Parkgrounds Inclosure, Matley Wood and Mark Ash. Because of their elusive nature, muntjac are easily overlooked and they may be far more numerous and widespread in the Forest than was realised. It seems likely that their numbers will build up further in the future although they may still seldom be seen by man.

Signs

In a particular habitat there is often a wide variety of signs which reveal not only the presence of deer but also their activities. A clue that deer frequent an area is provided by finding their tracks or *slot*. Deer produce tracks typical of cloven-hoofed animals, which in the New Forest also include cattle and pigs. The slot of deer are very much smaller and narrower than those of cattle and are narrower and more pointed than those of pigs. The size and shape of the tracks left by deer will depend on the species as well as gait, age, weight and sex of the individual concerned and the type of ground in which the impressions were made.

When moving from place to place, especially in dense cover, deer tend to travel in single-file along regular pathways. With a little

PRINTS OF CLOVEN HOOFED NEW FOREST ANIMALS

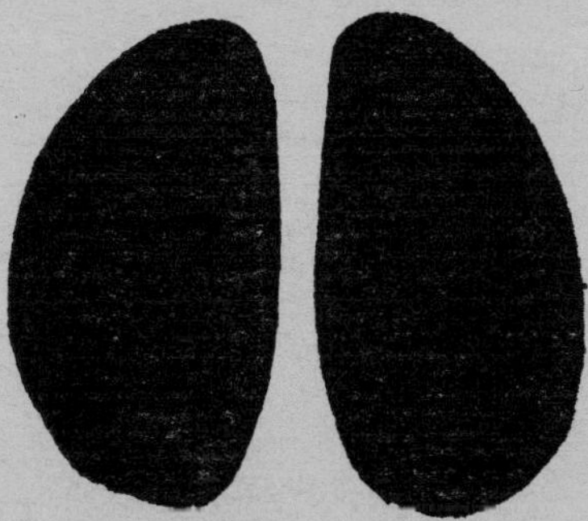

CATTLE

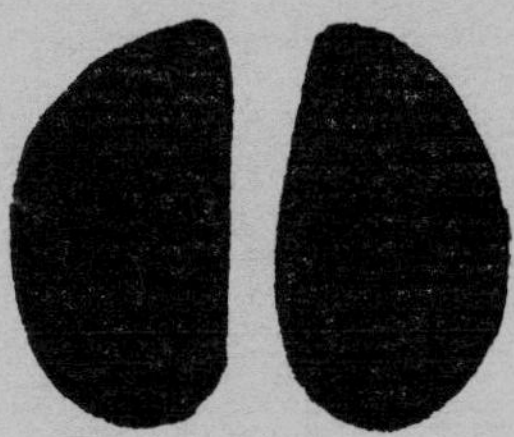

PIG

FALLOW DEER

DEER DROPPINGS

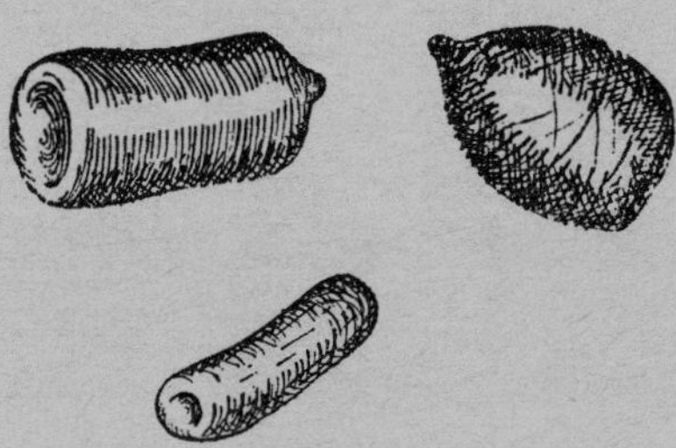

practice these paths are easy to find and when followed reveal substantial information on the animals' habits and favourite haunts. Such routes are especially clear where herds regularly cross damp ground or streams, slide down banks, cuttings or ditches, or encounter a fence or similar obstacle. Deer prefer to pass under a fence rather than jumping over; where a number of them regularly squeeze under such an obstacle, a depression or pass is quickly formed. In the Forest these are particularly obvious along the fenced edges of many Inclosures.

By following these paths the deer-watcher may come across lying-up areas where the animals settle down to rest or chew the cud. Their weight compresses the vegetation and compacts the soil, leaving tell-tale deer-sized impressions on the forest floor. Loose hair is commonly found in such sites, especially in spring when the winter coat is being shed. Piles of faeces are often deposited nearby but are voided elsewhere too. The droppings or *pellets* of deer are unlike those of any other animal in the New Forest. The shape, size, colour and consistency of the faeces will vary seasonally with the sex, condition and age of the animal and on the type of food taken, and it is extremely difficult, if not impossible, to deduce the species of deer from which the pellets originated. Deer normally defaecate 10–15 times a day.

Other indications that deer are active in an area can be obtained by examining the vegetation, especially trees and shrubs. In certain places, deer may browse woody vegetation. On the Open Forest it is difficult to tell whether they or the ponies and cattle are responsible for such damage; in the Inclosures, from which commonable animals are excluded but which deer use freely, there can be little reasonable doubt as to which animals have been browsing. As fresh new succulent growth is produced on trees and shrubs this is often plucked off and consumed by the deer. If this is done as soon as new buds break, the effect on the plant is akin to that produced by constant pruning or trimming of a bush or hedge. Where browsing is excessive, suppression of tree-growth may occur. Intensive long-term browsing may produce an effect similar to that of the ancient Japanese art of bonsai where trees are miniaturised by constant pruning. The small, stunted, dense bush-like growth form which results is particularly noticeable on beech, holly and hawthorn—all species commonly used by man for hedging. In other places, the attentions of deer may produce a browse-line. This happens where they have browsed up to the maximum height they can reach, thus suppressing growth of the woody vegetation, while above the browse-line normal luxuriant foliage is found.

Deer in the New Forest also fray, thrash, score and strip bark from trees. Further information on these activities are given in the Section on Population Trends, Damage and Deer Control.

Further evidence that deer are active in an area include *playrings*, *wallows* and *scrapes*. Playrings are formed by both roe and fallow where animals chase one another around a tree or bush while playing or during the rut. Scrapes are made during territorial and rutting behaviour where male deer scrape areas of ground bare, using the forefeet. Wallows are peaty or muddy hollows used by red and sika deer throughout the year and by them and by fallow bucks in the rut.

Watching

With the possible exception of the extreme south-eastern part, deer can regularly be found over the entire New Forest, although the distribution of sika and red deer is localised. Deer will visit most types of habitat during the course of the year but perhaps the most likely place to encounter these timid animals is along woodland edges. Although one may be fortunate enough to see deer at any hour of the daytime, especially during the winter, the best time to watch large numbers in the open is during the first and last hours of daylight.

Unless very lucky, one has to work hard in order to obtain reasonable views of deer. This can be a surprisingly exacting pastime, taxing both physically and mentally, although the majority of people find it worthwhile and very rewarding. The normal precautions employed when watching wildlife should be followed. Clothing should be of a sombre nature and made of material that does not rustle as you move. Footwear should also be dull-coloured, light-weight and silent. From the point of view of your own personal comfort it is advisable to cover as much skin as possible against the attentions of midges—this is also sound policy since the light-coloured skin of the human face and hands is very obvious from a long way off in woodland. Binoculars are an invaluable aid, especially the type with large front lenses as these have a greater light-gathering capacity than the human eye, producing a brightened image in dim light.

Deers' senses are exceptionally well developed. It is essential to remain as inconspicuous and silent as practicable when deer-watching. Ideally the observer should move so that the wind is blowing into the face, hence carrying his scent away from any animals ahead. The mark of a good deer-watcher is that not only can he or she approach and observe the animals undetected but can also depart without them ever being aware of his or her presence. Every effort should be made to avoid unduly upsetting these shy members of our fauna.

In summer, people sometimes come across appealing young spotted deer and misguidedly pick them up, believing that they have been orphaned or abandoned. This is rarely the case. Does and hinds naturally leave their newly-born offspring lying alone in cover during the day, only returning at intervals to suckle them. Therefore if you should find a fawn or calf *please* do not handle it: leave it safely where it is and depart quickly so as to avoid undue distress to the young animal or its mother, who will be watching you anxiously from nearby even though you may not see her.

When driving through the Forest one often sees deer. In such instances, the best way to watch them is to stop at a reasonable distance, provided of course that it is safe to do so, and study the animals from within the vehicle. Deer normally take far less notice of people inside cars than they do of those on foot. At night drivers must be especially careful as deer often panic when startled or blinded by the glare of car headlights.

Raised platforms or 'high seats' situated in strategic positions such as cross-rides and clearings will be seen in the Forest. These are used by keepers during census work and culling; on no account should they be used without Forestry Commission consent. The Commission have recently constructed three deer-observation hides where interested members of the public can watch and photograph wild sika, roe and fallow deer. These special hides may be used only by purchasing a permit in advance from the Queen's House, Lyndhurst.

For the less ardent or hardy person interested in deer and for the keen amateur photographer, a visit to the sanctuary at Bolderwood Farm is essential. This is located at the northern end of the Ornamental Drive between the A31 and A35 roads west of Lyndhurst. The sanctuary is a pocket of pastureland within the Forest to which, over the years, wild fallow bucks have been encouraged to come and graze undisturbed. The general public can watch the deer there but are forbidden to enter the fields themselves, and are asked to create as little disturbance as possible and not to take dogs with them. Information about the deer and an observation-platform are available. At certain times the bucks are fed on potatoes. Conducted visits to the sanctuary for parties should be organised well in advance through the Forestry Commission. There is a large car-park across the road at Bolderwood Green which is also the starting point for the Mark Ash nature trails.

Identification

The species of deer that live in the New Forest would seem to be unmistakable when compared in the textbook from the comfort of the armchair. In the field, the situation is often very different and even the expert may be uncertain of the identity of a particular animal in dense cover in the half-light of dawn or dusk. An important means of distinguishing between the species is on the basis of their relative sizes, colours and markings, especially those of the tail-region. Twice a year deer moult and change their coats. The thicker winter one is shed in late spring, often falling out in large chunks, and giving the animals a mangy appearance. In all the species, this moult involves a change in colour to a brighter, sleeker summer-coat which is retained until late autumn, when it is gradually replaced by the winter pelage again. Deer are born with a distinctive, well-spotted coat which provides camouflage during the first vulnerable weeks of life.

The descriptions given below are of typical animals and some deer may deviate appreciably from them. Coat-colour may vary considerably with the individual, with sex and age, whether the beast is wet or dry, on the lighting conditions or if the animal has been wallowing. Similarly, the size and weight of deer will also vary with a multitude of factors. The height given is that from the ground to the animal's shoulder; whole weights are used.

Red Deer

The red deer is the largest of the deer in the New Forest. Mature males, or stags, stand some 100–120 cm (40–48 in.) high and weigh approximately 122 kg (270 lb.). Females, or hinds, measure about 95 cm (37 in.) and weigh up to 73 kg (160 lb.). The winter-coat, which is dark brown with a varying amount of grey, is longer and coarser than in other species. The rich dark-red summer-coat is assumed in May. The tail is 15 cm (6 in.) long and the speculum, or caudal disc—a creamy patch across the rump—is less clearly defined than in sika, fallow, muntjac or roe deer. The underparts are also a light colour throughout the year. Mature stags have a prominent mane in winter. Young red deer, or calves, are born in June; they are spotted at birth but this baby-coat begins to be replaced after five or six weeks by a dull brown fluffy one.

Fallow Deer

Adult male fallow deer are called bucks, females does, and the young, fawns. In the New Forest the summer-coat is usually an attractive chestnut with prominent white spots, but in winter the spots are absent and the pelage is a very dark brown mulberry colour; the underparts are white all year. The tail in fallow is longer, 23 cm (9 in.) than that of any other British deer, and is flicked constantly in summer to ward off flies. A clear black line runs along the back to the tip of the tail and also borders the white rump-patch.

In the New Forest, a small proportion of the fallow are white. These are not albinos, merely a white variety. At birth, fawns of this type are dirty-white or sandy coloured, their coats becoming creamy-white by the next summer. There are also a small number of *menil*

RED

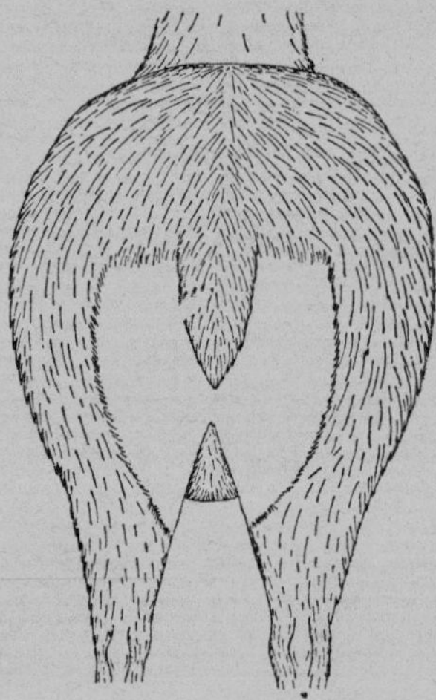

RUMPS OF NEW FOREST DEER

and black fallow in the New Forest. Unlike the common variety, menil fallow retain white spots in winter and the coat colour is generally paler. Black fallow are sooty brown in summer and slightly greyer in winter; the rump and whole tail-region are also this colour.

The weight of a prime buck may reach 90 kg (200 lb.); that of an adult doe at her best is normally 41–43 kg (90–95 lb.) although heavier individuals have been recorded. Fallow are smaller in stature than red deer, adult males being 90 cm (36 in.) tall and females 84 cm (33 in.); they are slightly larger and leggier than the sika.

Sika Deer

The summer-coat of the sika is a bright chestnut with yellowish-white spots, although these are fewer and less conspicuous than those of fallow deer at this season. Usually a clear row of white spots runs down either side of a dark dorsal stripe which follows the back-bone. The winter-coat is longer and darker in colour, being a sooty-brown above and grey-brown below; spots are normally absent.

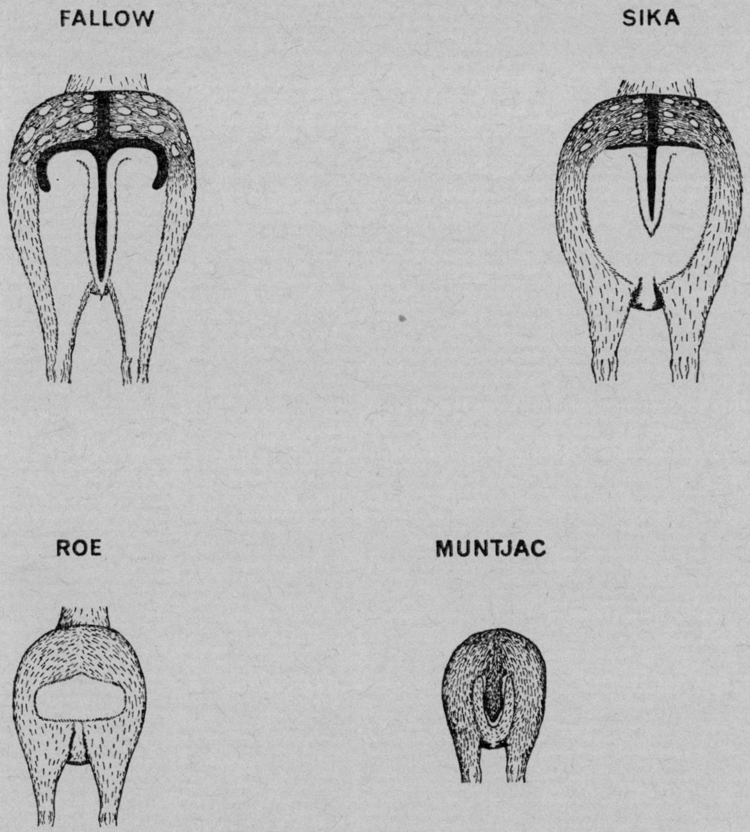

Stags, the males, are much darker than hinds, the females, and may appear black at a distance. The face is paler with a U-shaped lighter eyebrow-stripe or band which gives these deer a distinctive scowl. The rump-patch is white with a black edge and is conspicuous at all times of the year; it is often flared out when the deer are startled or fleeing. The tail of sika is 15 cm (6 in.) long, slightly shorter than that of fallow and usually has less black on the upper side. Young sika, called calves, are born in late May and June. Mature hinds are around 76 cm (30 in.) tall and weigh about 40 kg (88 lb.). Stags are larger and heavier, corresponding measurements being 80 cm (32 in.) and 64 kg (140 lb.).

Roe Deer
The summer-coat of roe deer is a bright foxy red-brown. The ears are large and black-bordered; the face is short and blunt, with a pale chin-patch, and in older animals is grey and grizzled. The rump-patch, or caudal disc, is buff coloured and lacks the black surrounds

shown by fallow and sika. In winter the pelage is grey-brown or grey and the caudal disc is conspicuously white; the rump hairs are erectile and are often flared out when the animal is alarmed. At this season the sexes can be distinguished by the shape of the white caudal disc, which is heart-shaped in does and kidney-shaped in bucks. Although does show a prominent white anal tuft of hair in winter there is no visible tail in roe, which distinguishes this species immediately from the other four. The young roe, called kids or fawns, are born in May. They are a light brown, flecked with white but this soon changes to a dull uniform brown; by October the young animal has a winter-coat like the adults.

A good New Forest roe buck will be 70 cm (28 in.) tall and weigh 25 kg (55 lb.); does are smaller, 65 cm (26 in.) high and 20 kg (45 lb.) in weight.

Muntjac

The muntjac is the smallest species of deer in the New Forest, mature adults standing 43–46 cm (17–18 in.) at the shoulder, although the rump is higher, and weighing 13–15 kg (30–35 lb.); there is little difference between the sizes of the sexes. From May until September the pelage is a rich sleek chestnut colour. The winter-coat, which is browner and greyer, is assumed by November. Underparts are lighter with white on the belly and the inside of the thighs. The forelegs are a darker brown on the front and sides and there is a lighter coloured throat-patch. The tail is 15 cm (6 in.) long, ginger on top and white underneath. When alarmed the deer hold their tails erect, fanning the white underside and also showing the white area round the anus. The diminutive fawns are spotted for the first eight weeks of life but unlike the other New Forest species muntjac may give birth in any month of the year.

Deer are capable of moving very stealthily and silently even in dense cover. With the exception of white fallow deer, all are able to merge into background cover remarkably well, often avoiding detection simply by standing still. The five New Forest species can all clear a 180-cm (6-ft) fence with comparative ease if pressed but normally prefer to pass under or through gaps in such obstacles. Sika, fallow, roe and red deer will all walk, trot, canter or gallop at times but each species has a typical characteristic gait which may be valuable for identification purposes. For example, red deer often travel in single file at a very rhythmic trot with the head held steady and erect. When suspicious of a strange object, such as a motionless observer, fallow may stand peering inquisitively at it or may show a behaviour-pattern known as stilting where they move with slow steps, lifting the feet high in an exaggerated manner like circus or dressage horses; in such circumstances the deer often stamp with the forefeet and bark to alert others. When alarmed, fallow are characteristically nervous, jumpy and indecisive; they will often bounce away on all four legs, with the tail raised vertically; if really frightened they will rush off immediately. Sika show bouncing and stilting gaits similar to fallow in the same circumstances; also they flare the white rump-patch when alarmed. Roe normally pick their way slowly and delicately through cover. When startled, roe characteristically bound away, barking, with the caudal-disc flared out. The gait of muntjac is characterised by the fact that they normally travel with the head lowered, and that the rump is higher than the shoulders.

Deer are normally silent for much of the time. The most vociferous species in the Forest are the roe and muntjac: both bucks and does of these species will readily utter a throaty, staccato dog-like bark of alarm, curiosity or excitement; territorial males may also bark to threaten or warn off intruding rivals. Both male and female fallow and red deer may give short, gruff barks when uneasy but unable to identify the source of potential danger; in similar situations sika whistle or squeal. Mothers and young of all species communicate by a variety of plaintive bleating or 'peeping' sounds. In moments of extreme stress, all deer can produce loud, anguished shrieks. During the rut the male deer become highly vociferous.

Antlers

One of the most conspicuous and interesting features of deer is their antlers. With the exception of reindeer, in which they are often present in both sexes, and the antler-less Chinese water- and musk-deer, only the males normally carry antlers. They are secondary sexual characteristics, serving both as weapons and as symbols of rank or social status. The deciduous antlers of deer have a different structure from the true horns of animals such as cattle and antelope. Horns are permanent structures comprised of a central core of living bone with a hard outer covering of *keratin*, the substances of which claws and hooves are also made. Although antlers are also composed of bone, these are shed and re-grown annually. They originate from two raised portions of the skull known as pedicels, situated just above and behind the eye-sockets. Growing antlers need nutrients. Internally these are supplied through blood-vessels running up from the pedicel to ramify through the new bone-tissue. Developing antlers are covered externally by soft furry skin or velvet which also contains blood-vessels.

Each set or 'head' of antlers takes four to five months to grow and during this period the male is said to be 'in velvet'. As antler-development proceeds, a thicker ring of bone known as the coronet forms at the junction of pedicel and antler. When the antler is fully grown the velvet is shed, the process being accelerated by the

PRICKET

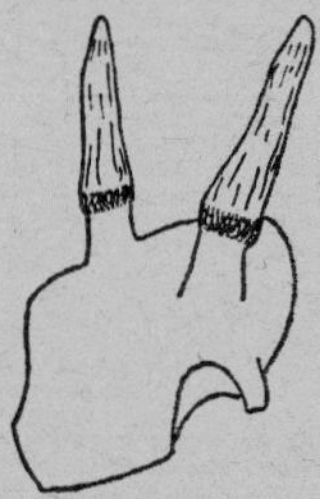

SOREL

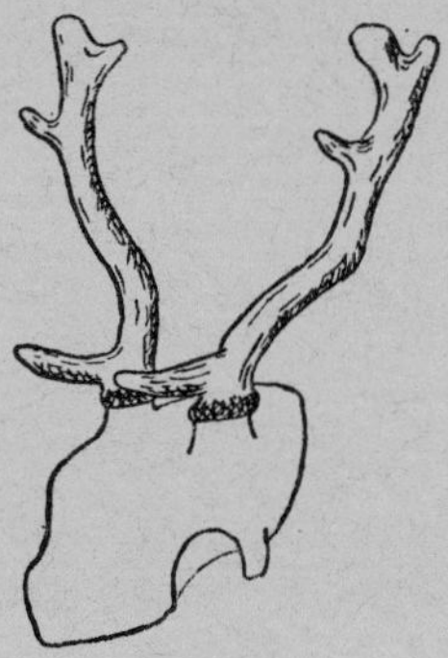

BUCK

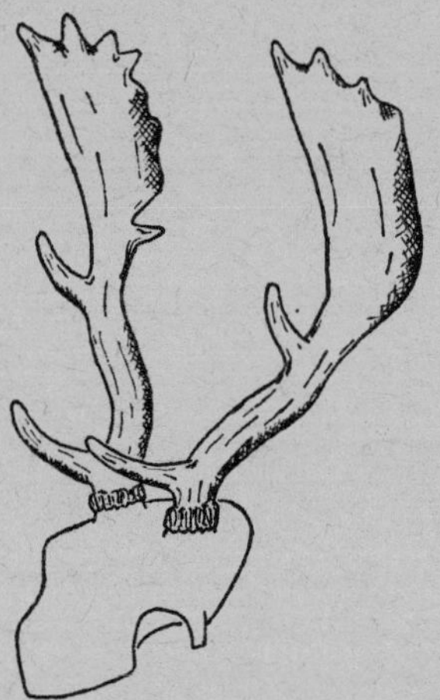

TYPICAL ANTLER DEVELOPMENT

animals rubbing or fraying their now hard antlers against suitable fraying-stocks such as young pliable-trees. The males are now said to be in 'hard-antler' or, misleadingly, 'hard-horn'. Initially the freshly cleaned antlers are light coloured but continued rubbing against vegetation produces a darkened burnished effect. Deer carry their hard antlers for about eight months of the year. At the end of this period the dead antler quickly loosens at its base on the pedicel

SORE

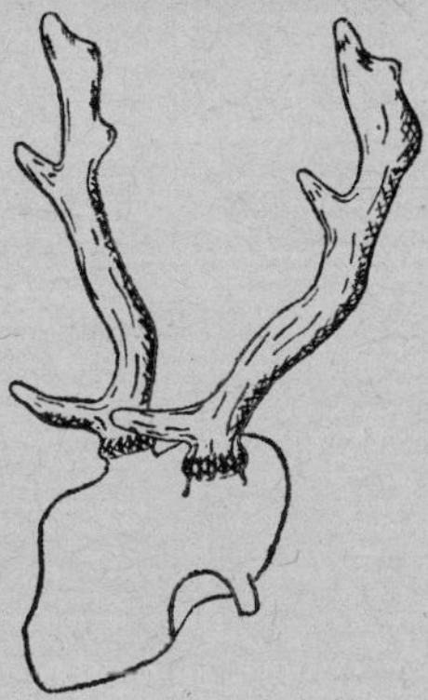

BARE BUCK

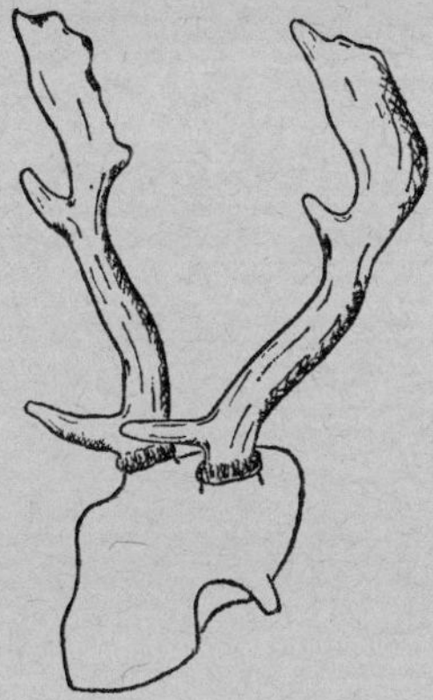

GREAT BUCK

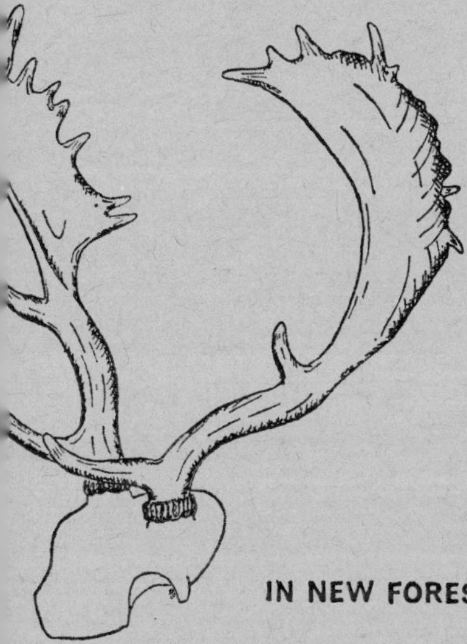

IN NEW FOREST FALLOW DEER

and falls or is knocked-off. Growth of the new head of antlers then starts within a few days of casting.

The annual cycle of antler-growth and casting is hormonally controlled and largely follows the male reproductive cycle so that they are in hard-antler during the period of the year when they are fertile. Fallow, sika and red deer show similar seasonal antler-development. The previous year's antlers are cast in spring—red deer about March, fallow and sika in April; younger animals often cast after the older ones. During the summer the new antler grows in its coat of velvet; in August and September the blood-supply constricts, the velvet dries and is removed by fraying. The new pair of antlers is now ready for the rigours of the coming mating season. Roe differ in that they cast their antlers in November or December; the new set of antlers is grown during the winter months and cleaned by early May. Muntjac males also grow a new set of antlers annually but unlike the other species in the Forest they breed in all months of the year, so that at any particular season some bucks are in hard-antler whereas others are still in various stages of velvet.

The first head of antlers grown by deer, normally started during the first year of life, are small, simple unbranched spikes. In subsequent years, each new pair of antlers may become larger and more complex until the best set is produced in prime adult life. In elderly males that have passed their best, the subsequent size and quality of the antlers often declines and they are said to be 'going back'. Antler size, shape and the age at which the best head is produced will vary from animal to animal, between species and with the quality and quantity of the food available. Antlers are therefore not necessarily a good indication of a deer's age.

In sika, roe and red deer, the antlers are of a classical branching shape, form and developmental pattern. Fallow are distinct from the other four New Forest species in that the parts of the antler furthest from the skull are flattened and palmated in mature individuals. Muntjac have only short simple spike-like antlers, rarely ever exceeding 7.5 cm (3 in.) in length, which are borne on prominent hairy pedicels of a similar length. However, the male muntjac do have large, prominent upper canine teeth up to 4 cm (1.5 in.) long which may be used in fighting between rival bucks (*see* plate 4).

A rich terminology, involving a variety of regional dialects, is used in Great Britain in describing the approximate age of male deer on the dubious basis of antler-size and form. In the New Forest, male deer of all species with their first head of antlers are called *prickets*, although young sika are often termed *knobbers* and young red deer *brockets*. Fallow then progress to a *sorel* (second head), *sore*, *barebuck*, *buck* and *great buck*. Heads of sika, roe and red deer are normally described on the basis of the combined number of points or tines on the antlers.

Being made of bone, antlers are comparatively rich in calcium and phosphorus, and once cast the deer may chew them to obtain quantities of these essential nutrients. However, one may be fortunate enough to find cast antlers although it needs a keen eye to spot them in ground vegetation as they look remarkably like dead branches.

Breeding

Although fallow, sika and red deer are capable of breeding successfully for a period of about six months in every year, mating is normally concentrated into a shorter distinctive rutting season. In many areas of the Forest, mature males of these three species live apart from the females and juveniles for much of the year but during the late summer and early autumn the sexes intermingle in preparation for the rut. By then the males are in hard antler, the Adam's apple is swollen and the neck is large and heavy. Stags and bucks become increasingly restive and aggressive, beginning to fray, thrash and anoint trees and bushes, also rolling and wallowing in scrapes in which they urinate. During this period, males develop a strong musty rutting-odour which is distinctive for each species.

Fallow and sika use traditional areas, where the dominant or master males mark out their territories or rutting-stands. As sexual activity builds up the males begin to call. Fallow bucks groan, a throaty grunting noise difficult to describe in words but unmistakable when heard. Sika stags characteristically whistle, repeating this call three or four times. Large numbers of deer may congregate in the vicinity of the stands and as does and hinds come into season they are served by territorial males.

Red deer differ from sika and fallow in that the stags gather harems of hinds together which they then follow around and defend against rivals. The roar of the red stag is most often heard in September and October.

Serious fights between rival males of approximately equal size and status occur only infrequently and are rarely lethal although always spectacular. During the rut males of sika, fallow and red deer feed only furtively and with the rigours of mating their physical reserves are quickly depleted. They may then be forced by exhaustion to retire from the stands or relinquish their harems. The master-stag or buck's place is then taken by the next animal in the male hierarchy.

During the rut a variety of soft calling sounds are made between males and females. If females are not mated or covered successfully when they first come on to heat, they will become receptive again in about three weeks time and late matings may occur. The gestation period in sika, fallow and red deer is approximately eight months, calves and fawns being born around the following June, although late matings result in late births.

Unlike the fallow, sika and red deer in the Forest, roe are not normally gregarious. From April onwards, when they are in hard antler, bucks begin to establish their territories. These may be as much as 12 hectares (30 acres) in size, depending upon the type of vegetation, the terrain and the social standing of the buck concerned. Territorial boundaries are denoted by the resident male fraying, thrashing and anointing small trees with the antlers, and making scrapes in the soil or on the boles of trees using the fore-feet. Important scent glands are situated on the forehead between the antlers, and between the cleaves of the hooves. The bucks' treatment of trees and bushes therefore leaves both visual and olfactory signs to ward off potential intruders. In addition, the resident buck may patrol the limits of his domain, barking to deter other males from entering it. Some fighting between rivals occurs and is considerably more vicious and less ritualised than that of larger deer species.

Once the roe bucks have established their territories, they normally live entirely within them for the duration of the summer. Does are also territorial to a lesser extent. Generally roe pair up in summer although cases of polygamy are known. The doe is on heat for only two days but during this time the buck chivvies her ceaselessly, often chasing her around specific landmarks, thus forming well worn 'roe-rings'. The rut falls sometime between mid-June and mid-August when fertilisation occurs. A second bout of sexual activity, the false-rut, may occur in October.

Roe display a remarkable feature known as delayed implantation whereby the ova fertilised in the summer lie dormant in the mother until late December when they then resume normal development. The kids or fawns are born in the following May; about two-thirds of the roe does in the New Forest bear twins.

Muntjac differ from the other four species of deer in the Forest in breeding continuously, each doe giving birth to a fawn about every seven months. Within a few days of dropping her fawn the doe will copulate and the development of the new embryo starts immediately. Fawns may be born in any month of the year. Like roe deer, muntjac are also territorial, marking out the boundaries of their domains by fraying and anointing small saplings, scraping the ground and depositing heaps of droppings.

Herds

Fallow, sika and red deer are predominantly gregarious, herd-living animals. For much of the year mature males live apart from the females and juveniles, which in the New Forest are known as 'small-deer', only returning to the latter's areas for the rut though sometimes then remaining until late winter when herds range further afield in search of food. Herd-size and composition vary with both the time of year and the species concerned. Deer in open areas such as moor and grasslands tend to form larger herds than their woodland-dwelling counterparts. The true size of herds is often difficult to determine as several smaller groups may amalgamate to form one large aggregation when using common feeding-grounds; the smaller units are then reformed as the animals leave the area. This is especially true of sika.

In the frequently adverse conditions of late winter and early spring when food is scarcest, large herds of up to 30 fallow does and juveniles form, particularly in poorer habitats such as moorland. By mid-May these herds split up and pregnant females are often solitary by the time the fallow fawns are born in June; herds gradually reform by the rut in October. These small-deer herds are matriarchal, generally being led by an experienced adult doe; male-deer herds appear to be less closely knit associations.

Herds of sika in the Forest are generally smaller than those of fallow. The situation as regards red deer is difficult to judge as so few live in the New Forest. For much of the year roe deer are strictly territorial although, in winter, small herds of up to five animals are occasionally encountered. Little is known about muntjac; some authors say they are solitary deer while others suggest they live in small family-associations of up to four animals.

Food

A thorough understanding of the feeding-habits of deer in different situations is important, especially when considering correct stocking rates, improvement of deer habitat and the causes and methods of prevention of damage to forestry, agricultural and horticultural concerns.

Between 1970 and 1973 an intensive study was carried out into the feeding-habits of the fallow and roe in the New Forest. This was achieved by intensive observation of wild animals, supported by examination of stomach-contents from over 450 animals which had been either culled, or killed in road accidents.

The diet of fallow in the Forest during the year can be divided into three phases; the importance, duration and timing of these change with locality, climate and from year to year. From about March until September, sweet grasses are the main food, with herbs and browse from deciduous trees being of minor importance. This period may extend into early November in years when there is a poor acorn-crop but in those years when the nuts are plentiful they form the primary food from September until Christmas. Winter foods include bramble, bilberry, sweet grasses, ling-heather, holly, ivy, and browse from felled conifers. The third phase runs from the time that the autumnal nut-crop is exhausted until the appearance of the new growth or 'bite' of grass in March or April. In common with other deer, fallow are highly selective when feeding. Plants that are abundant in the Forest but are rarely eaten by them include bracken, purple moorgrass, bristle bent-grass and the bell-heathers; gorse is not browsed to any significant extent in mild winters.

Where sweet grasses form the staple diet of fallow for much of the year, bramble and rose fill this role in the roe which browse to a far greater degree than do the fallow, sika and red deer in the Forest. Young succulent shoots are avidly sought out. During the winter, coniferous browse and ivy are major foods, together with bramble; in March and April, quantities of heather and bilberry are also eaten. Grasses are of some importance in the summer when, besides bramble and rose, large amounts of new herbs and shoots from broadleaved trees are eaten. In the autumn, fungi and acorns are sought after. Various other mosses and ferns are taken but form an insignificant part of their diet.

The feeding habits of sika, muntjac and red deer were not studied. It is said that the New Forest sika browse more than do other populations of this species elsewhere in Britain; their diet in the Forest probably resembles that of the fallow described above. Studies on red-deer diet in habitats in other parts of Europe similar to the New Forest suggest that the population in this part of Hampshire will also take the same types of foods as do fallow there. Muntjac are predominantly browsers, taking a varied diet in which ivy, bramble, grass and acorns are prominent.

Parasites and Disease

At present our knowledge of the health of deer in this country is incomplete although much progress has been made in recent years. The two commonest ectoparasites on deer in the New Forest are the sheep or castor-bean tick (*Ixodes ricinus*) and the deer ked (*Lipoptena cervi*); both these small arthropods live on the hosts and feed on their blood. A recent survey revealed that ticks and keds were present on practically every fallow and roe deer examined in the Forest, being found in greatest abundance in the summer or on sick or debilitated animals. The tick is a potentially important transmitter of various diseases which could infect deer in the British Isles, including red-water and tickborne fevers and perhaps the virus of louping ill. Species of lice are occasionally taken from Forest deer and are probably much commoner than is realised as they are easily over-looked due to their small size.

A commonly recorded endoparasite is the liver-fluke (*Fasciola hepatica*). In the New Forest there seems to be a much higher incidence of this parasite in fallow than in roe; sika seem largely unaffected. However in only a small proportion of the fallow herds does liver-fluke become serious, the vast majority of deer suffering only minor infections. In roe deer, infection of the lungs with roundworms (*Dictyocaulus* sp.) may result in parasitic pneumonia which can cause appreciable mortality. Foot-and-mouth disease has so far never been detected in any freeliving British deer even though they are often in close contact with domestic stock.

Various congenital abnormalities have been recorded in New Forest herds, the most bizarre of which was a red deer born without eyes or eyesockets. Antler abnormalities may occur through physical damage or disease. In areas near main roads a small percentage of the deer population suffer from malformed limbs where bones, having been broken in road accidents, have set incorrectly or lower limbs have withered and fallen off. Generally, however, the health of the deer in the Forest is good. With the exception of roe, few deer are found dead from disease.

Population Trends, Damage and Deer Control

The three basic factors governing changes in the sizes of animal populations are birth, death and immigration or emigration.

Let us firstly consider the effects of immigration and emigration on deer numbers in the New Forest. Deer can and do leave the area to intermingle with other feral herds in neighbouring parts of Hampshire and Wiltshire. When individuals leave the Forest permanently they have effectively gone from the breeding stock and represent a loss in terms of deer numbers. But it is equally true that animals from these neighbouring herds may enter the Forest to swell the numbers there. For a number of years, culling of deer, especially fallow, on estates and farms adjoining Crown Land has often been ruthlessly carried out. In such situations this means that the numbers of deer leaving the comparative protection of the Inclosures and Open Forest far exceeds that of those re-entering it. Hence there is a tendency for the stocks of deer in peripheral areas of the New Forest to fall as a result of heavy shooting on the adjacent private land.

Death obviously results in a decline in the population, and a variety of agencies take their toll of deer. Nowadays there are no large carnivores in the Forest which would attack adult animals although foxes may take a number of newly-born or weak fawns, calves or kids. Roe deer, particularly when young, are susceptible to parasitic pneumonia, but otherwise New Forest deer are remarkably healthy animals and deaths through disease are minimal. In the 13-year period from 1962 to the end of 1974 a total of 673 dead deer, mainly fallow and roe, were recovered as a result of road-traffic accidents in the Forest. Many other collisions are not reported by motorists and the maimed deer may wander away to die later from their injuries. Especially at night, drivers should keep a close watch for animals on both fenced and unfenced roads as both deer and commonable stock show little road-sense; some accident black-spots are marked by warning road signs. All road accidents involving deer or domestic stock in the New Forest should be reported to the local police.

In recent years, poaching has posed an increasing menace to deer herds and accounts for the grizzly deaths of an unknown number of animals. Many of the techniques poachers employ involve immeasurable cruelty and can only be described as barbaric. They include the use of wire snares, spot-lights, long-dogs such as lurchers or greyhound crosses to pull down deer, and guns of unsuitable calibre or power. The revulsion felt on finding a deer maimed or killed in such a manner is indescribable. The co-operation of the public in immediately reporting any suspicious activity to the police would help to eradicate poaching in the Forest. However, the police strongly advise people against taking personal action against poachers.

In the favourable conditions provided by the New Forest, fallow does breed annually, first conceiving when about 16 months old and bearing a single fawn. With the existing sex-ratio and age-structure, the fallow population in the Forest can potentially increase by one third per annum. Sika hinds also produce a single calf each year and their rate of multiplication will match that of fallow. About 70 per cent of roe does on Crown Land bear twins although many of these die in the early weeks of life. The potential rate of increase of the red and muntjac are not known precisely.

We must now consider the overall balance-sheet for deer in the Forest. Although factors such as road accidents, disease and poaching account for the death of a number of individuals each year, this figure is far outweighed by the population-increase due to births. Thus under the present circumstances the overall number of deer in the New Forest would increase at an appreciable rate if it were allowed to do so. For a variety of reasons it is essential at the moment for man to regulate the stocks of deer on the Crown Land. Animals injured in road accidents or by poachers must be destroyed as quickly and humanely as possible, as should those which are diseased, weak or very old. If this is not done the health and well-being of the entire stock might be endangered and the injured deer would otherwise suffer long, lingering and often painful deaths.

Timber-production is an important industry in the New Forest and deer may damage trees in a variety of ways. Saplings of suitable size and flexibility are used by male deer firstly to rub the velvet off their fully grown antlers and then to polish or burnish them. Such behaviour removes bark from the fraying stocks which will suppress their growth and increase the risk of fungal infection. If the bark is removed in a complete ring or girdle round the trunk then the tree will die. Roe and muntjac bucks are particularly noted for such activity as they mark out their territories. Male deer may also thrash trees and other vegetation during the mating season. Young trees are again often the target for such shows of aggression which, although an impressive display of the animal's power, is looked on in a different light by the forester.

At certain times of the year, notably in late winter and early spring, bark-stripping may occur. In the New Forest this activity is confined primarily to fallow and sika. The reasons for it are complex and not fully understood; tree-bark may be taken as roughage, for its mineral content, as a means of regulating digestion or due to stress. Bark-stripping is confined to certain species of tree; some, such as holly, are of little forestry importance but the effects on conifers is the same as that of fraying. Deer remove bark by digging the front teeth of their lower jaw into the tree, levering up a small portion which is then gripped in the mouth and wrenched upwards. Deer may also damage large trees by scoring or gouging them, using the tips of the antlers; sika stags in New Copse, Frame and Stockley are particularly prone to this habit. Constant browsing by deer may also distort, kill or suppress growth of trees planted for timber.

Although a certain degree of deer-damage to forestry concerns is tolerated, a level may be reached where it becomes no longer economically acceptable. In the long-term, changes in forestry practice may alleviate the situation, but if substantial damage is occurring then a quick solution is needed. Two main remedies exist; firstly, the susceptible trees can be fenced off but this is an expensive process which also denies deer access to other natural foods growing abundantly there. Secondly, shooting the individuals or ring-leaders causing the trouble can be carried out.

Besides sometimes damaging growing timber, deer may also enter nearby fields, gardens or horticultural concerns to feed. This is unpopular with many local landowners and tenants and persistently offending animals frequently have to be shot.

A given habitat is only capable of sustaining a certain number of healthy deer. If this limit or carrying capacity is exceeded, as might happen if the number of deer were not kept in check by culling, both the animals and their environment would suffer, as has occurred for example in parts of New Zealand. The ultimate limiting factor in the New Forest would probably be food-supply, although the incidence of disease would also increase as the deer became crowded. Each area offers only a certain finite amount of food; if too many animals are dependent on this limited supply, deaths through starvation and malnutrition will result, especially in hard winters—as happened to the deer in the New Forest in the Middle Ages. Therefore it is considered better to control the number of deer, firstly to maintain a healthy stock rather than have large numbers of poorer quality animals, and secondly to keep the amount of damage they do to an acceptable level.

All shooting of deer in England and Wales is controlled by the 1963 Deer Act; Scotland has its own laws. This Act lays down strict regulations on such matters as the type of rifle to be used and the close seasons to be observed. Besides this, the Forestry Commission has its own additional stringent regulations. Not only does the Commission carefully work out the number, sex and approximate age of deer to be culled each year, but also often lists specific animals to be shot in areas where excessive damage has or is liable to occur. The actual shooting is done by Forestry Commission marksmen, highly skilled in this work. Culled animals are eviscerated and sold to the local butcher for human consumption; the quality of New Forest venison is generally first-class. In some areas deer are shot by local landowners when the animals enter their fields.

Deer have been hunted with hounds in the New Forest for many centuries. Since the First World War the one remaining pack, the New Forest Buckhounds, has hunted only male fallow. Their season starts in early September and continues throughout that month; no hunting take place in October because of the rut but it recommences in early November and goes on until April. The buckhounds, which are slightly larger than foxhounds, hunt on two days a week, Monday and Friday. Hunt officials wear green jackets. The kennels are at New Park near Brockenhurst. Hunting is selective and emphasis is laid on taking any injured or sick animals; on quite a number of days towards the end of the hunting-season the hounds are used simply to break up large herds and move them away from situations where they are doing damage to crops or gardens. In recent years the number of bucks killed during the season rarely reached double figures.

The deer in the New Forest should not be thought of as simply a liability. Proper management, integrating deer in relation to forestry and agriculture, can yield valuable cash-returns from the sale of venison and stalking rights. As with all wildlife, deer have an intrinsic aesthetic beauty which is immeasurable in economic terms. They are an integral part of the New Forest heritage—in fact it will be recalled that the Forest was first set up in order that royalty could hunt this quarry.

Bibliography

Cadman, W. A. *The Fallow Deer.* Forestry Commission Leaflet no. 52. HMSO, London, 1966.

Chard, J. S. R. *The Roe Deer.* Forestry Commission Forest Record no. 99. HMSO, London, 1974.

Delap, P. (ed.). Deer in Britain Series. 1: *Fallow Deer*, N. & D. Chapman; 2: *Muntjac*, O. Dansie; 3: *Sika Deer*, M. T. Horwood & E. H. Masters; 4: *Roe Deer*, P. Delap; 5: *Red Deer*, P. Delap. British Deer Society, 1970.

Harris, R. A. & Duff, K. R. *Wild Deer in Britain*. David & Charles, Newton Abbot, 1970.

Prior, R. *Living with Deer*. Andre Deutsch, London, 1965.

Prior, R. *The Roe Deer of Cranborne Chase*. Oxford University Press, London, 1968.

Southern, H. N. (ed.). *The Handbook of British Mammals*. Blackwell Scientific Publications, Oxford, 1964.

Taylor Page, F. J. (ed.). *Field Guide to British Deer*. Blackwell Scientific Publications, Oxford, 1971.

Whitehead, G. K. *The Deer of Great Britain and Ireland*. Routledge & Kegan Paul, London, 1964.

Addresses

Forestry Commission, Queen's House, Lyndhurst, Hampshire SO4 7NH. Lyndhurst 2801.

Nature Conservancy Council, Shrubbs Hill Road, Lyndhurst, Hampshire SO4 7DJ. Lyndhurst 2840.

Police Station, Lyndhurst, Hampshire SO4 7NR. Lyndhurst 2813.

British Deer Society, Riverside House, Heytesbury, Warminster, Wiltshire BA12 0HF.

Mammal Society, Harvest House, 62 London Road, Reading, Berkshire RG1 5AS.

1. A magnificent Red deer stag

2. Red deer at Burley in December. Stag and hinds with a calf in the centre foreground.

4 (*opposite*). An adult Muntjac buck. The short antlers and protruding upper canine tooth are characteristic. *M. Clark*

3. A watchful Roe doe

5. A mature Sika stag showing his white rump patch

6. Sika hind at Frame

7. A Roe doe in tall grass. The black nose is characteristic.

8. A young Roe buck in July

9. Red deer stags: note the mane, pale rump and short tail.

10. Fallow buck in April. The well-palmated antlers will soon be cast.

11. A white Fallow buck in winter, feeding on gorse.

12. Fallow bucks, white and common varieties, fighting during the rut in October.

13 (*opposite*). A 10-pointer Red deer stag feeding on heather

14. A young fawn. Many species of deer have a spotted coat at birth.

16 (*opposite*). Up and over. A Fallow deer leaping a fence.

15. Fallow bucks, white and common, at Bolderwood.

17. Red deer stag in winter coat

19 (*opposite*). Silka stag in winter. New Copse.

18. Troubled by flies. Fallow bucks in summer, with partly grown antlers.

20. Fallow bucks at Bolderwood with their antlers, almost fully grown, in 'velvet'.

21. A rutting Fallow buck depositing scent from his suborbital glands on a beech tree

22. Fallow deer frequent fields as well as woods

23. A sandy-coloured Fallow fawn with a common Fallow doe showing her distinctive tail markings.

24. A menil Fallow doe in summer coat. Young conifer plantations provide seclusion.